NARCISSISTIC ABUSE RECOVERY FOR BLACKS

Healing Trauma, Reclaiming Power, and Building Resilience within the Black Community

GBOGO .S. ADEGBOYE

1

INTRODUCTION

Welcome to "Narcissistic Abuse Recovery for Blacks," a transformative guidebook designed specifically for Black individuals who have experienced the devastating effects of narcissistic abuse. In the pages that follow, we embark on a journey of healing, empowerment, and reclaiming personal power in the face of trauma and adversity. Narcissistic abuse is a pervasive and insidious form of manipulation and control that can have profound and long-lasting effects on its survivors. For Black individuals, navigating the complexities of narcissistic abuse can be compounded by cultural factors, systemic inequalities, and intergenerational trauma, making the journey to recovery even more challenging.

In this book, we delve into the unique challenges faced by Black survivors of narcissistic abuse, exploring the intersection of race, culture, and trauma. We examine the impact of generational trauma, cultural barriers to seeking support, and societal stereotypes about mental health within the Black community. Through compelling storytelling, evidence-based techniques, and actionable advice, we provide a comprehensive roadmap for healing, growth, and transformation. Throughout these pages, you will find insights, tools, and strategies to help you navigate every stage of the recovery journey. From defining narcissistic abuse and understanding its impact to setting boundaries, rebuilding trust in relationships, and finding meaning in the journey of recovery, we offer guidance and support every step of the way. Moreover, "Narcissistic Abuse Recovery for Blacks" is more than just a book – it is a beacon of hope, validation, and empowerment for Black individuals seeking to reclaim their sense of self-worth, dignity, and resilience. Through stories of resilience and triumph, advocacy for systemic change, and resources for building supportive networks and communities, we empower you to break free from the chains of abuse and create a life of healing, empowerment, and purpose.

Whether you are a survivor of narcissistic abuse, a friend or family member seeking to support a loved one, or a mental health professional working with Black individuals, this book is a valuable resource for healing and empowerment. With its compassionate approach, culturally competent insights, and empowering message of resilience and hope, "Narcissistic Abuse Recovery for Blacks" is a guidebook for reclaiming your power and rewriting your story. Welcome to the journey of healing and empowerment.

Chapter One

WHAT IS NARCISSISTIC ABUSE

Narcissistic abuse is a sequence of actions meant to undermine the victim's belief in reality, autonomy, and self-worth. When someone has narcissistic personality traits or narcissistic personality disorder (NPD), they can manipulate and dominate others psychologically through a subtle and sophisticated process known as narcissistic abuse. It happens in a variety of interactions, such as friendships, family ties, romantic partnerships, and work relationships. Knowing the nature of narcissism is essential to understanding narcissistic abuse. An exaggerated sense of one's own significance, an incessant need for approval, and a lack of empathy for others are traits associated with narcissism. People who exhibit narcissistic qualities frequently use control and authority over others around them in an effort to uphold their superior self-image.

Narcissistic abuse can take many different forms, and its victims are frequently left feeling bewildered, alone, and emotionally destroyed. Typical strategies used by narcissistic abusers include:

1. Gaslighting: Denying or manipulating facts, events, or feelings in order to manipulate the victim's perception of reality. The victim of gaslighting begins to doubt their perceptions and doubt their own sanity.

2. Emotional manipulation: influencing the victim's ideas, feelings, and actions by instilling in them feelings of guilt, shame, and fear. Frequently, this manipulation entails taking advantage of weaknesses and fears.

3. Devaluation and discard: Initially idealizing the victim, but as their value or admiration dwindles, devaluing and discarding them. The

victim may experience severe emotional distress as a result of this cycle of idealization, devaluation, and discard.

4. Isolation: Removing the victim from resources, friends, or family in order to keep them in control of their thoughts and behaviour. Being alone increases the abuser's power and makes it harder for the victim to get assistance.

5. **Projection:** Blaming the victim for the abuser's own shortcomings, mistakes, or abusive behaviours. This diverts attention from the abuser's actions and avoids taking responsibility.

6. Coercive control: Using coercion, threats, or resource manipulation to establish authority and control over the victim. The victim's freedom and autonomy are restricted by coercive control, making it more difficult for them to leave the abusive situation.

It can be difficult for victims to identify and acknowledge narcissistic abuse because it is not always obvious and can be subtle. Moreover, societal misconceptions about abuse often lead victims to blame themselves or downplay their experiences.

It's crucial to recognize that narcissistic abuse is not a reflection of the victim's inadequacies or weaknesses but rather a manifestation of the abuser's dysfunctional behaviour and distorted worldview. Recovery from narcissistic abuse involves reclaiming one's sense of self, rebuilding boundaries, and seeking support from qualified professionals and empathetic allies.

Understanding the dynamics of narcissistic abuse and its impact on victims, we can work towards creating safer and more supportive environments where individuals can heal and thrive.

A widespread kind of psychological manipulation and control, narcissistic abuse has a lasting impact on Black families and individuals, casting a lengthy shadow over the community. Its influence extends beyond interpersonal interactions and is intricately entwined with societal, historical, and cultural factors, influencing the fundamental fabric of Black communal life.

The wounds left by historical traumas like enslavement, segregation, and persistent structural racism within the Black community provide an ideal environment for the seeds of narcissistic abuse to germinate and flourish. A complex web of vulnerabilities has been created by the history of oppression, which has impacted interpersonal interactions and exacerbated power imbalances. Moreover, a lot of people are discouraged from getting treatment or simply admitting they have been abused because of societal stigmas and preconceptions about mental health and therapy. The situation is made more complex by inter-sectionality, which arises from Black people navigating several axes of oppression and identity. The confluence of race, gender, and sexual orientation, for example, might increase the likelihood of abuse for Black LGBTQ+ people and make it more difficult for them to find assistance in societies that might not be open to recognizing other identities. Although they are frequently a source of resilience and strength, community institutions can also act as havens for abuse. Close-knit family ties and cultural expectations of allegiance may unintentionally protect offenders and keep victims quiet, thereby sustaining trauma and secrecy cycles. As a result, a lot of survivors experience isolation, struggle with emotions of guilt and betrayal, and are unable to get the help they so sorely need. Black survivors of narcissistic abuse suffer additional difficulties due to economic inequality and restricted access to supports. These differences are exacerbated by the lack of culturally competent mental health treatments, which leaves many people unable to get the help they need to become well.

The Black community is a symbol of resiliency and resistance in the face of hardship despite these enormous challenges. All those affected by narcissistic abuse must have access to culturally affirming assistance, be empowered to recover their agency, and confront oppressive structures in order to promote healing and safer environments. To put it simply, generating empathy, solidarity, and significant change requires a knowledge of the complex ways that narcissistic abuse connects with the Black experience. We may start to demolish the systems that support abuse and foster communities of healing and freedom by addressing these problems head-on and pushing for culturally sensitive interventions.

➢ SOME IMPORTANCE OF RECOVERY AND HEALING

1. **Psychological Well-Being**: Following narcissistic abuse, psychological well-being must be restored by healing and recovery. Numerous mental health conditions, such as sadness, anxiety, PTSD, and low self-esteem, are frequently experienced by victims. Healing enables people to deal with these problems and reclaim stability and inner serenity.

2. **Breaking the Cycle**: For a lot of survivors, ending the abuse cycle is crucial. In addition to assisting people in leaving violent

relationships behind, healing also keeps them from repeating negative behaviors in new partnerships. It gives individuals the ability to spot warning signs and set sensible boundaries for their own safety.

3. **Reclaiming Identity**: Victims of narcissistic abuse frequently experience a sense of disorientation and disconnection from their identity. Reclaiming and regaining one's identity, values, and goals is a necessary part of recovery. It enables people to recover a strong sense of self-worth and autonomy while escaping the gaslighting and manipulation of the abuser.

4. **Rebuilding Trust**: Victims of narcissistic abuse may lose faith in both themselves and other people. Rebuilding trust in oneself, other people, and the wider world is a necessary part of healing. It calls for

developing the ability to separate healthy relationships from unhealthy ones and progressively becoming more receptive to sincere connections with reliable people.

5. **Physical Health**: The effects of narcissistic abuse can be seen on the body in addition to the mind. Survivors frequently have chronic stress, sleep difficulties, and other health problems. Through lowering stress levels, enhancing the quality of sleep, and promoting general health and vigor, recovery and healing enhance physical well-being.

6. **Empowerment**: Getting well gives survivors the ability to reclaim their lives and futures. It entails realizing one's own power, resiliency, and potential for development. Healing teaches people how to confidently state their needs and desires, create boundaries, and speak up for themselves.

7. **Effect on Future Relationships**:

Unresolved trauma resulting from narcissistic abuse can have a detrimental effect on subsequent relationships, causing pain and dysfunction to repeat again. For future romantic, familial, or platonic relationships to have healthy dynamics, healing is necessary. It enables people to approach relationships with transparency, sincerity, and confidence.

8. **Effect on Children and Generations**:

Healing for parents who have experienced abuse is not just about their personal health but also about ending the abuse cycle for future generations. Parents who heal themselves can provide a healthier atmosphere for their kids, giving them safe attachments and excellent role models.

9. **Social Contribution**: Recovering from narcissistic abuse enables people to make

constructive contributions to both their local communities and society as a whole. Survivors who are empowered and healed are better able to promote social change, increase public awareness of abuse, and assist others in their healing processes.

Narcissistic abuse recovery and healing are essential for regaining mental and physical health, ending the abuse cycle, regaining identity and trust, empowering survivors, building wholesome relationships, and having a positive influence on coming generations and society at large.

Chapter Two

UNDERSTANDING NARCISSISM AND NARCISSISTIC PERSONALITY DISORDER (NPD)

A complicated and frequently harmful psychological pattern, narcissistic attitudes and behaviours are defined by an obsessive fixation with oneself, a sense of entitlement, a lack of empathy for others, and an ongoing desire for validation and admiration. Recognizing and managing relationships with people who display narcissistic tendencies requires an understanding of these characteristics and actions. An exaggerated feeling of grandiosity and self-importance is the fundamental component of narcissistic personality traits. People who exhibit narcissistic qualities believe they are better than other people and want particular attention and respect from those around them. This grandiose self-image hides deep-seated flaws beneath a façade of confidence and arrogance, acting as a shield against emotions of inadequacy and insecurity.

An overwhelming sense of entitlement is another feature of narcissistic conduct. Narcissists frequently disregard the needs and boundaries of others in their belief that they are naturally deserving of special treatment, consideration, and recognition. They could have little concern for other people's feelings or well-being and instead take advantage of or manipulate those around them to satisfy their own needs.

The absence of empathy and sympathy for other people is a characteristic that sets narcissistic people apart. They perceive others as nothing more than tools to be used for their own gain and find it difficult to identify or comprehend the feelings and viewpoints of those around them. Because they lack empathy, narcissists can take advantage of and manipulate people without feeling guilty or regretting it, advancing their own goals at the expense of the people they come into contact with. A fundamental component of narcissistic conduct is an unwavering desire for approval and affirmation from others. Adulation and attention are what narcissists need to support their shaky self-esteem and affirm their inflated sense of who they are. To satisfy their ravenous ego and preserve their sense of superiority, they could act in attention-seeking ways like bragging, inflating their accomplishments, or pursuing attention and approval.

Even with their outward shows of assurance and confidence, narcissists frequently suffer from guilt and deep-seated insecurities. Beneath their haughty exterior, there is a frail ego that is easily hurt by rejection or perceived criticism. When faced with challenges to their self-worth, narcissists may react defensively, using manipulative strategies, or withdraw into a victim mentality in order to save their delicate sense of identity. Grandiosity, entitlement, a lack of empathy, and a persistent desire for approval are only a few of the complex interactions that make up narcissistic traits and behaviours. Knowing these characteristics is crucial for spotting and interacting with narcissistic people, figuring out the weaknesses hiding behind their façade of confidence, and shielding oneself from the negative consequences of their deceptive actions.

➢ CHARACTERISTICS OF INDIVIDUAL WITH NPD

1. **Grandiosity:** - People with NPD frequently have an excessive sense of significance in themselves and may think they are better than other people. In an attempt to maintain their inflated sense of self-worth, they frequently embellish their

accomplishments and abilities.

2. **Lack of Empathy:** Narcissists find it difficult to identify or comprehend the feelings and viewpoints of others. They could put their own demands and wants before of everyone else's, dismissing or being unaffected by the emotions of others around them.

3. **Need for Admiration:** Individuals with NPD are constantly in need of other people's approval and attention. To support their shaky sense of self-worth and maintain their superiority complex, they are continuously looking for validation and praise.

4. **Sense of Entitlement:** Narcissists frequently think they have a right to preferential treatment or benefits. They can assume that others would take care of their wants and requirements without thinking about other people's feelings or personal space.

5. **Manipulative Behaviour:** - Narcissists usually

use manipulative strategies to further their objectives or hold onto power over others. They might take advantage of people and circumstances by charming, flattering, or lying.

6. **Shallow Relationships:** - Narcissists frequently find it difficult to build genuine, meaningful ties with people, despite their need for adoration. Instead of real emotional closeness, their relationships are usually transactional and surface-level, driven by what others can do for them.

7. **Intolerance of Criticism or Rejection:** People with NPD tend to have low self-esteem and are extremely sensitive to slights or criticism. When their accomplishments or abilities are questioned, they could respond violently or defensively.

8. **Hostility and Envy:** - Narcissists may feel jealous of others who they consider to be more admirable or accomplished. When faced with those they perceive as challenges to their supremacy or

sense of self, they could react with hatred or disdain.

9. **Fantasies of Power and Success:** - Narcissists frequently harbor extravagant ideas of unrestricted success, brilliance, or power. They could boast excessively about their skills or achievements because they think they are born winners and should be given preferential treatment.

10. **Difficulty with Intimate Relationships:** Narcissists find it difficult to be truly intimate and vulnerable emotionally, despite their seeming confidence. Their relationships are frequently marked by control, manipulation, and a lack of empathy, which causes friction and discontentment on a regular basis.

Together, these traits add to the intricate and frequently harmful interpersonal dynamics seen in partnerships with people who suffer from narcissistic personality disorder. Recognizing and negotiating relationships with narcissistic people while defending one's own limits and well-being requires an understanding of these characteristics. Narcissism has a significant and wide-ranging effect on relationships and societies, affecting not just individual interactions but also more general social dynamics. Narcissistic people frequently leave a path of devastation in their wake, hurting the people who are closest to them and adding to the dysfunction of the greater community. Narcissism in close relationships can result in a wide range of difficulties and disputes. Because narcissists put their own demands and wants above all else, their partners may become victims of emotional abuse, manipulation, and gaslighting. Because of the narcissist's grandiosity and lack of empathy, authentic emotional connection is hindered, which damages intimacy and trust. As partners try to negotiate the rough seas of a relationship with a narcissist, they may eventually suffer from low self-esteem, anxiety, and despair. Because they are shallow and exploitative by nature, narcissistic people frequently find it difficult to keep up lasting relationships. They could go through phases of dating, ending things with people who don't meet their needs or don't give them the kind of respect and recognition they want. Former lovers are left hurt and disillusioned by this process of idealization, devaluation, and discarding, which leaves a path of emotional misery in its wake.

Beyond personal relationships, narcissism has an impact on larger communities and social systems. Narcissistic parents can produce poisonous situations in their families that are marked by emotional neglect, partiality, and manipulation. Raised by narcissistic parents, children frequently suffer from severe emotional trauma and struggle with codependency, low self-esteem, and trouble establishing meaningful relationships as adults.

In work environments, narcissistic people can damage collaboration, upset team dynamics, and put their own growth ahead of the organization's success. Their desire for approval and affirmation might push them into immoral actions like stealing credit for other people's labor or deceiving coworkers for their own benefit. This may result in a hostile workplace full of distrust, rivalry, and animosity.

Social cohesiveness and trust can be undermined by the pervasiveness of narcissism, which also fosters an individualistic and self-serving culture. Empathy and compassion may be lacking in narcissistic groups, which exacerbates social alienation and division. Furthermore, the normalizing of narcissistic conduct in popular culture and the media may support dysfunctional interpersonal dynamics and negative stereotypes.

Developing empathy and emotional intelligence, supporting individuals impacted by narcissistic abuse, and increasing awareness are all important components of a multidimensional strategy to address the effects of narcissism on relationships and communities. Communities may lessen the negative impacts of narcissism and create stronger, more durable relationships by promoting a culture of respect for one another, cooperation, and sincere connection.

Chapter Three

RECOGNIZING NARCISSISTIC ABUSE IN BLACK RELATIONSHIPS

Within various nations and communities, the dynamics of narcissistic abuse are shaped in large part by cultural variables. The perception, acceptance, and handling of narcissistic conduct are shaped by cultural norms, beliefs, and expectations. These factors ultimately determine the frequency and significance of narcissistic abuse in a given cultural setting. An aspect of culture that shapes the dynamics of narcissistic abuse is the preference for collectivism over individualism. Group cohesion and adherence to social standards may be given more importance in cultures that value collectivism, such as many Asian and African countries. People may find it challenging to confront authoritative persons, especially narcissistic abusers, or to speak out against abusive behaviour because to this emphasis on group well-being. Victims may experience pressure to put the demands of the group before their personal welfare, which could result in abuse being silenced and accepted as the norm.

On the other hand, cultures that value individualism—like many Western societies—may unintentionally create conditions that encourage the prevalence and tolerance of narcissistic behaviour. Emphasizing one's own accomplishments and successes can feed narcissistic tendencies like entitlement and grandiosity. Narcissistic people may be more inclined in these societies to take advantage of other people for their own benefit and put their own wants ahead of those of others, which fosters an environment of individualistic rivalry and self-interest.

Narcissistic abuse dynamics are also influenced by cultural ideas around gender roles and power dynamics. Narcissistic men may utilize coercion and manipulation to maintain control over their partners and families in patriarchal society, where men possess a disproportionate amount of power and authority. Additionally, it may be challenging for female victims of abuse to confront or leave abusive relationships due to traditional gender standards that demand subservience and obedience from women.

The stigma associated with mental health and therapy in our culture can also be a deterrent to getting treatment for narcissistic abuse. Victims may feel embarrassed or hesitant to share their experiences of abuse or seek treatment from mental health specialists in cultures where mental illness is stigmatized or seen as a sign of weakness. This stigma has the potential to exacerbate feelings of loneliness and keep people from getting the help they require to become well.

Within cultural contexts, religious and spiritual beliefs also influence the dynamics of narcissistic abuse. In societies where religious or spiritual leaders have considerable power and influence, victims might be dissuaded from asking for assistance or coming forward to report mistreatment committed by individuals in positions of authority. Spiritual teachings that place a strong emphasis on submission and forgiveness can also be used to excuse abusive behaviour and dissuade victims from standing up for themselves or fighting for justice.

The dynamics of narcissistic abuse within various nations and communities are significantly influenced by cultural factors. Communities can endeavour to create conditions that support victims, confront abusive behaviour, and foster respectful, healthy relationships by acknowledging and addressing these cultural effects.

➤ Myths and misconceptions about abuse in Black relationships

Myths and false beliefs regarding violence in Black relationships impede attempts to address and prevent domestic violence in the community, silence survivors, and reinforce negative stereotypes. By looking into and dispelling these myths, we may encourage a better knowledge, awareness, and support system for those who have experienced trauma.

1. Myth: Abuse only occurs in Black relationships. - Reality: Domestic violence affects people of all racial and ethnic backgrounds. However, there's a chance that underreporting of abuse in the Black community is a result of cultural issues like stigma, fear of judgment, and mistrust of law enforcement.

2. Myth: Black women cannot be abused because they are naturally strong and tough. - Reality: Although the Black community values strength and perseverance, these qualities do not shield a person

from abuse. Because they fear being viewed as weak or unable, Black women may be discouraged from asking for assistance or talking about their experiences of abuse due to stereotypes about their strength.

3. Myth: Abuse is something personal that belongs only in the family. - Reality: Domestic abuse is a problem that affects people individually, in families, and in communities. Hiding abuse results in cycles of violence and keeps victims from getting the help and resources they require to get well.

4. Myth: Black males are naturally violent and abusive. - Reality: Although there are Black men who abuse women and children, it is unjust and damaging to maintain stereotypes that vilify an entire community based on the behavior of a small number of people. This myth undercuts attempts to address domestic abuse holistically and ignores the variety of identities and experiences within the Black community.

5. Myth: Abuse only happens in heterosexual

relationships. - Reality: Relationships including people of any gender identity or sexual orientation can experience domestic violence. The Black community may provide particular difficulties for LGBTQ+ people seeking resources and support because of stigma, discrimination, and a dearth of services that are culturally sensitive.

6. Myth: Abuse isn't really abuse if it's not physical. - Reality: Abuse can be financial, emotional, psychological, or sexual in nature. Abuse that is not physical can still be harmful and can have long-lasting damage to the mental and emotional health of survivors.

7. Myth: Abuse victims need to have done something to their abuser. - Reality: Regardless of one's behavior or actions, no one deserves to be harmed. Victim-blaming mindsets reinforce negative stereotypes and transfer blame from the offender to the victim, which makes it more difficult for survivors to ask for assistance and support.

It will take a concentrated effort to advance cultural

competency, education, and awareness inside and outside of the Black community in order to dispel these myths and misconceptions. Through encouraging candid communication, offering assistance, and pushing for legislative modifications, we can establish more secure and encouraging spaces where victims of domestic abuse can come forward, recover, and prosper.

Chapter Four

THE PSYCHOLOGICAL IMPACT OF NARCISSISTIC ABUSE

Narcissistic abuse has severe and long-lasting impacts on a victim's emotional and mental health, frequently leaving scars long after the abuse has stopped. In contrast to physical abuse, which results in obvious wounds, narcissistic abuse frequently causes invisible but just as severe harm.

The victim's sense of value and self-esteem are severely damaged as a result of narcissistic abuse. The abuser's constant manipulation, gaslighting, and criticism can cause the victim to question their own value, feelings, and views. This can eventually result in self-loathing, guilt, and feelings of inadequacy, which makes it harder for the victim to trust their own judgment or to assert themselves.

The mental health of the victim of narcissistic abuse is also negatively impacted, frequently resulting in anxiety, sadness, and complex posttraumatic stress disorder (C-PTSD). The combination of the unpredictable and volatile conduct of the abuser and the ongoing stress of living in an abusive situation can cause hypervigilance, flashbacks, and trouble controlling emotions. In an attempt to break free from the abusive cycle, victims may struggle with ongoing feelings of fear, helplessness, and hopelessness.

Furthermore, the victim's relationships with other people may be significantly impacted by narcissistic abuse. Victims may avoid social situations because of fear of being judged or rejected, or they may find it difficult to establish and keep up positive relationships because of trust concerns and a vulnerability-related worry. The psychological scars from narcissistic abuse can also hinder a victim's capacity to be a good parent, which can harm their kids' mental health and continue abusive cycles across generations.

Beyond the short-term impacts on emotional and mental health, narcissistic abuse can have long-term ramifications on the general well-being and quality of life of survivors. Numerous survivors report continuing difficulties with problems like low self-esteem, trouble establishing boundaries, and difficulties establishing close relationships. Some people may try to numb the pain or retake control by using harmful coping techniques, like substance misuse or self-harm.

It is critical to understand that recovering from narcissistic abuse is a difficult, non-linear process that calls for patience, understanding, and self-compassion. On their path to recovery and healing, survivors may find great value in counseling, support groups, and self-care routines. Safer, more supportive societies where survivors can heal and prosper can be achieved by confronting social attitudes that diminish or trivialize abuse, recognizing survivors' experiences, and offering compassionate assistance.

Coping mechanisms and defence mechanisms commonly observed in victims

In order to survive in the face of continual trauma and manipulation, victims of narcissistic abuse frequently adopt coping and defines mechanisms. Although these tactics are adaptive reactions to the abusive environment, they may also have long-term negative effects on the person's relationships and emotional health.

Dissociation is a typical coping strategy used by victims of narcissistic abuse. Dissociation is the process of separating oneself from reality in an attempt to cope with the overwhelming agony and trauma of abuse. During abusive episodes, victims may dissociate, mentally removing themselves from the situation in an effort to shield themselves from the severity of the emotions. Dissociation might offer momentary solace, but it can also result in feelings of alienation from oneself and other people, which makes it challenging to manage emotions and build wholesome relationships.

Denying or downplaying the maltreatment is an additional coping strategy. In an effort to retain control over their circumstances and avoid acknowledging the terrible truth of their predicament, victims may minimize the severity of the abuse or persuade themselves that they deserve the maltreatment. Denial can act as a coping strategy for victims of abuse, enabling them to carry on with their everyday activities in spite of the trauma they are going through.

Some victims of abuse by narcissists become hypervigilant in an attempt to defend themselves. Hypervigilance entails being on the lookout for threats or indications of danger all the time, predicting the abuser's next move, and adjusting one's conduct to prevent inciting their wrath or revenge. Hypervigilance can cause chronic worry, anxiety, and tiredness as victims stay on high alert all the time, even if it may help victims manage the unpredictable nature of narcissistic abuse.

To make meaning of their experiences and reclaim power, victims may also absorb the abuser's negative messages or engage in self-blame. Feelings of shame, remorse, and self-loathing may be sustained if they think they are somehow to blame for the abuse or that they are undeserving of love and respect. The victim may find it difficult to speak out for themselves or to fight for their needs as a result of these damaging self-beliefs, which can have a significant impact on their sense of self-worth and self-image.

Coping strategies frequently have a negative impact on the emotional and psychological health of the victim of narcissistic abuse, even though they can offer momentary solace from its suffering. In order to establish better coping strategies and manage their healing journey, victims must be aware of the effects of these coping mechanisms and seek support from reliable friends, family members, or mental health experts. It is possible to establish a more secure and encouraging atmosphere for victims of narcissistic abuse to recover and flourish by acknowledging and valuing the experiences of survivors, offering compassionate assistance, and confronting detrimental attitudes and actions.

Breaking the cycle of trauma and healing psychological wounds
Ending the traumatizing cycle and mending the psychological scars left by narcissistic abuse is a difficult and multidimensional process that calls for

bravery, resiliency, and assistance. It entails realizing the effects of the abuse, recognizing unhealthy coping mechanisms, and creating more positive relationships with oneself and other people.

Acknowledging and comprehending the mechanisms of narcissistic abuse is essential to ending the trauma cycle. This entails identifying the abusive actions and strategies used by the narcissist and comprehending the effects these actions have had on the person's relationships, identity, and feeling of self-worth. Survivors can regain their agency and power in the healing process by having their experiences validated and the harm caused by the abuse acknowledged.

Another crucial element in recovering from narcissistic abuse is self-compassion. Because of the abuse, survivors frequently experience feelings of humiliation, guilt, and inadequacy. Treating oneself with love, understanding, and acceptance— regardless of one's prior experiences or perceived shortcomings—is a key component in practicing self-compassion. It is admitting with empathy one's own anguish and suffering and realizing that no one should be subjected to brutality or contempt.

When trying to recover from narcissistic abuse, survivors may find that therapy and counseling are quite helpful. In therapy, victims can process their feelings, analyse their experiences, and create coping mechanisms to deal with the aftereffects of the abuse in a secure and encouraging setting. Counsellors can assist survivors in recognizing unhealthy thought and behaviour patterns, challenging self-defeating attitudes, and creating more positive interpersonal relationships.

Creating a network of friends, family, and peers who are supportive can also help with the healing process after narcissistic abuse. Making connections with people who have gone through comparable things might help to lessen feelings of loneliness and isolation by offering validation, empathy, and understanding. When navigating their healing journey, survivors must surround themselves with individuals who respect and acknowledge their experiences, validate their feelings, and offer them unconditional support.

Holistic self-care techniques, in addition to individual therapy and support systems, can be extremely important in the healing process following narcissistic abuse. Exercise, meditation, writing, and other pursuits that enhance one's physical, mental, and spiritual well-being can assist survivors in re-establishing a connection with oneself as well as developing resilience and inner serenity. Important components of self-care and healing include prioritizing one's needs, setting limits, and using assertiveness.

In the end, ending the traumatizing cycle and mending psychological scars from narcissistic abuse is a slow, continuous process that calls for perseverance, self-compassion, and dedication. In the wake of abuse, survivors may rebuild their lives, recover their sense of self-worth, and create better, more satisfying relationships by admitting their experiences, getting assistance, and practicing self-care.

Chapter Five

HEALING FROM NARCISSISTIC ABUSE

The cornerstones of recovery from narcissistic abuse are self-care and self-compassion, which give survivors the vital resources they need to mend and start again. Following abuse, victims frequently experience intense emotions of guilt, worthlessness, and self-doubt. Resilience, self-worth, and emotional well-being can be fostered by engaging in self-care and self-compassion practices, which can help offset these negative feelings.

Giving survivors a sense of agency and control over their lives is one of the main advantages of self-care. Survivors of narcissistic abuse frequently have a sense of helplessness and helplessness, believing that their needs and boundaries are continuously disregarded by the abuser. By taking care of their bodies, minds, and emotions, survivors can regain control over their lives and become stronger advocates for themselves and their needs.

In addition, self-care is essential for controlling

emotions and stress. Because of the trauma they have experienced, survivors of narcissistic abuse may have elevated levels of anxiety, despair, and hypervigilance. Exercise, mindfulness, and relaxation techniques are examples of self-care activities that can help balance and calm the body and mind while also calming the nervous system and lowering the effects of stress hormones.

Additionally, self-care encourages physical vigor and health, which are sometimes overlooked in the wake of abuse. The physical health of survivors of narcissistic abuse can be negatively impacted, resulting in conditions like chronic pain, immunological malfunction, and insomnia. Making self-care a priority can strengthen immunity, boost energy, and improve general well-being. Examples of self-care activities include regular exercise, a healthy diet, and getting enough sleep.

Healing from narcissistic abuse requires developing self-compassion in addition to self-care. Being kind, understanding, and accepting of oneself is a key component of self-compassion, especially during times of sorrow, anguish, and self-doubt.

Because of the abuse, victims of narcissistic abuse frequently experience emotions of guilt, inadequacy, and self-blame. Recognizing that no one deserves to be treated unfairly or minimized entails facing these uncomfortable feelings with empathy and compassion when engaging in self-compassion practices.

In order to practice self-compassion, one must also question one's own self-perceptions and swap them out for narratives that are more affirming and compassionate. Survivors may absorb the abuser's comments and come to feel that they are undeserving of happiness, respect, or affection. It is necessary to confront these damaging ideas and acknowledge one's innate value and dignity as a human being in order to cultivate self-compassion.

In the end, self-care and self-compassion are crucial elements of narcissistic abuse recovery, giving survivors the strength, confidence, and support they require to mend and start again. In the wake of abuse, survivors can regain their sense of self-worth, restore their self-esteem, and create healthier, more satisfying relationships by putting their well-being first, engaging in self-care, and developing self-compassion.

Steps to initiate the healing process
1. Acknowledge the Abuse: Recognizing and recognizing that there was narcissistic abuse is the first step toward recovery. This entails identifying the narcissist's abusive actions and strategies as well as their effects on your mental and emotional health.

2. Seek Support: Speak with dependable family members, friends, or support groups for understanding, empathy, and affirmation. Making connections with people who have gone through comparable circumstances can make you feel less alone and offer insightful opinions and insights into your healing process.

3. Educate Yourself : Find out about the characteristics of narcissistic abuse as well as the typical characteristics and actions of narcissistic people. You can better make sense of your experiences and identify similar dynamics in future

relationships by being aware of the abuse patterns.

4. Set Boundaries: To shield oneself from additional abuse and exploitation, set up distinct boundaries. This could entail putting an end to or restricting interactions with the narcissist, establishing boundaries for interaction and communication, and firmly stating your requirements and preferences.

5. Practice Self-Care: Make self-care and self-compassion your top priorities by giving your physical, emotional, and mental health the attention they deserve. Exercise, journaling, meditation, creative expression, and time spent in nature are a few examples of this. Seek out pursuits that uplift your spirit and provide you with happiness and relaxation.

6. Seek Professional Help: You might want to think about going to therapy or counseling with a licensed mental health practitioner who specializes in helping victims of narcissistic abuse. You can process your feelings, explore your experiences, and create coping mechanisms to deal with the

aftereffects of the abuse in a safe and encouraging environment in therapy.

7. Challenge Negative Self-Beliefs: Recognize and confront any internalized messages and negative self-beliefs that you may have picked up from the abuse. Change these damaging ideas with narratives that are kinder and more affirming of your intrinsic value as a person.

8. Practice Forgiveness (of Yourself): Acknowledge that you are not to blame for the abuse and forgive yourself for any perceived transgressions or failings. Give up on self-blame, guilt, and humiliation and instead concentrate on developing self-compassion and self-understanding.

9. Set Realistic Expectations: Recognize that recovery from narcissistic abuse is a patient, progressive, and nonlinear process that requires time. Have reasonable goals for yourself and give yourself permission to move forward at your own speed without criticism or coercion.

10. Showcase Personal Development: Make the most of your chance for self-improvement and self-learning by using the experience of narcissistic abuse. Consider the things you have gained from the experience and decide which aspects of your life you would like to develop further.

In the wake of narcissistic abuse, you can start to regain your sense of self-worth, rebuild your self-esteem, and create better, more meaningful relationships by following these steps to start the healing process.

Setting boundaries and reclaiming personal power

Regaining personal control and establishing boundaries are crucial steps in recovering from narcissistic abuse. Regaining your own authority can seem like an overwhelming effort if you have been the victim of abuse, especially if it came from a narcissist who routinely crossed your boundaries and abused your feeling of autonomy. Nonetheless, it is a crucial stage in the healing process and in reestablishing one's feeling of agency and self-worth.

Establishing boundaries entails stating your right to be treated with decency and respect as well as being transparent with others about your needs, preferences, and limitations. Setting boundaries can be difficult or even frightening for those who have experienced narcissistic abuse at first because it means going against deeply ingrained patterns of self-doubt and people-pleasing behavior. Regaining your own power, however, entails realizing that you have the authority to put your health first and set boundaries—even if doing so offends people or encounters opposition.

Overcoming guilt, shame, and self-doubt is a major obstacle to setting boundaries following narcissistic abuse. It's possible that survivors internalized the abuser's teachings and came to feel unloved, unrespected, and unconsidered. Because they worry that they are being unreasonable or selfish, people may experience shame or self-blame when they set limits. But it's crucial to understand that establishing boundaries is an act of self-preservation and care rather than selfishness. Regaining control over your ideas, feelings, and behaviors is another aspect of regaining your own power. It's possible that victims of narcissistic abuse were socialized to put the abuser's wants and demands ahead of their own, which robbed them of their identity and autonomy. Reclaiming personal authority is stating your right to make decisions that are consistent with your values and objectives and realizing that you are not accountable for the ideas, feelings, or deeds of other people.

Regaining personal authority and establishing boundaries need engaging in self-compassion practices. It entails being compassionate, understanding, and accepting of yourself, especially when you're struggling or feeling self-conscious. Acknowledge that establishing boundaries might be difficult at times, and that it's acceptable to ask for help from dependable family members, friends, or mental health specialists while you work through this process.

In the end, regaining personal control and establishing boundaries are transforming expressions of self-love and self-respect. You can clearly communicate to yourself and others that you are deserving of love, respect, and consideration by setting boundaries. It is a significant step toward recovering your sense of agency and self-worth in life as well as healing from narcissistic abuse.

Chapter Six

OVERCOMING SHAME AND STIGMA IN SEEKING HELP

In order to guarantee that victims of narcissistic abuse, especially those from marginalized communities, have access to the tools and help they require to heal and rehabilitate, it is imperative that cultural barriers to seeking care be addressed. Cultural barriers can include the stigma associated with mental health, mistrust of authoritative figures, family and community customs, and ignorance of the support options that are accessible.

The stigma that surrounds mental health in many communities is a major cultural obstacle to getting support. Some cultures stigmatize mental illness as a moral failing or a show of weakness, which makes people reluctant to get treatment. If narcissistic abuse survivors talk about their experiences or get therapy, they could fear criticism or social rejection. Raising awareness of mental health issues, dispelling damaging assumptions, and spreading messages of acceptance, compassion, and support are all necessary to combat this stigma.

Mistrust of institutions and authority figures is another cultural barrier, especially among communities that have traditionally been subjected to systemic discrimination and oppression. For fear of being retraumatized or suffering unfavorable outcomes, survivors may be reluctant to seek assistance from social agencies, law enforcement, or mental health specialists. Establishing rapport and trust with survivors demands culturally competent methods that put an emphasis on validation, empathy, and understanding of their experiences.

The willingness of survivors to seek support may also be influenced by cultural norms around the family and community. Maintaining family unity and loyalty in the face of abuse or dysfunction is highly valued in many cultures. Survivors may worry that if they talk about their experiences or ask for assistance from someone outside of their family, they will be shunned or held responsible by them. Establishing safe spaces where survivors can talk candidly about their experiences without fear of rejection or retaliation is necessary to challenge these societal norms.

Furthermore, in some places, there might not be enough knowledge about the resources and support services that are accessible. Survivors might not be aware of their rights and alternatives, or they might not know where to turn for assistance. Improving the availability of information and resources via culturally appropriate channels, including community centers, religious institutions, or ethnic media, can aid in closing this gap and guaranteeing that survivors receive the assistance they require.

In summary, removing cultural obstacles to getting help necessitates a multipronged strategy that includes promoting awareness, fostering trust, combating stigma, and expanding access to services that are culturally competent. We can guarantee that victims of narcissistic abuse from all walks of life get the help and resources they require to recover and thrive by building networks of care that are inclusive and sensitive to cultural differences.

Challenging societal stereotypes about mental health in the Black community

Challenging societal stereotypes about mental health in the Black community is crucial for creating a more inclusive and supportive environment where individuals feel empowered to seek help and access the resources they need to heal and thrive. Historically, mental health issues have been stigmatized and marginalized within many communities, including the Black community, leading to underreporting, misdiagnosis, and inadequate treatment of mental health conditions.

One of the most pervasive stereotypes about mental health in the Black community is the idea that seeking help for mental health issues is a sign of weakness or moral failing. This stereotype is rooted in historical traumas such as slavery, segregation, and systemic racism, which have fostered a culture of resilience and self-reliance within the Black community. As a result, individuals may feel pressure to "tough it out" or "pray it away" rather than seeking professional help for mental health concerns.

Another stereotype is the belief that mental health issues are a result of personal weakness or character flaws, rather than legitimate medical conditions. This stereotype can lead to feelings of shame, guilt, and self-blame among individuals struggling with mental health issues, making it difficult for them to seek help or disclose their experiences to others. Addressing this stereotype requires education and awareness about the biological, psychological, and social factors that contribute to mental health conditions.

Moreover, there is a pervasive stereotype within the Black community that mental health issues are a "White" problem and not relevant to people of color. This stereotype is perpetuated by systemic disparities in access to mental health care, including lack of culturally competent services, underrepresentation of Black mental health professionals, and mistrust of the medical establishment due to historical trauma and discrimination. Challenging this stereotype requires increasing access to culturally relevant mental health resources and services, as well as promoting representation and diversity within the mental health profession.

Additionally, there is a stereotype that mental health issues are a source of shame and weakness that should be kept hidden from others. This stigma can prevent individuals from seeking help or disclosing their experiences to friends, family members, or employers, out of fear of judgment or rejection. Challenging this stigma requires creating safe spaces where individuals feel comfortable speaking openly about their mental health concerns, as well as promoting messages of acceptance, understanding, and support.

Challenging societal stereotypes about mental health in the Black community requires a concerted effort to promote education, awareness, and cultural competence. By addressing stigma, increasing access to resources, and promoting representation and diversity within the mental health profession, we can create a more inclusive and supportive environment where individuals feel empowered to prioritize their mental health and seek help when needed.

➢ Finding culturally competent therapists and
   resources

For people to receive efficient and encouraging
mental health care, especially those from
underrepresented areas, they must locate culturally
competent therapists and resources. Therapists who
are able to integrate culturally appropriate
techniques into their practice and who recognize
and value the identities, experiences, and cultural
origins of their clients are practicing culturally
competent therapy.

A difficulty encountered by people looking for
culturally competent therapy is the lack of diversity
in the mental health field. Many therapists might
not be aware of or sensitive to their clients' distinct
cultural experiences and viewpoints, which can
result in misunderstandings, poor treatment, and
miscommunication. It is imperative that people
look for therapists who are devoted to continuing
their education and training in cultural competency,
as well as who have experience working with a
variety of communities.

Thankfully, there are a number of resources
available to assist people in locating mental health

treatments and therapists that are culturally competent. One way to find therapists who specialize in working with various populations is to ask reliable community organizations, religious leaders, or healthcare providers for recommendations. These sources might be able to offer suggestions based on what they know about the training, experience, and therapeutic style of the therapist.

Online databases and directories can also be quite helpful for those looking for therapists who are culturally competent. Therapists who specialize in working with Black and Latinx groups can be found in directories on websites like Therapy for Black Girls, Therapy for Black Men, and Therapy for Latinx. These directories make it simpler for people to identify therapists who suit their unique needs and preferences by frequently including information about the training, specializations, and treatment philosophies of therapists.

Asking therapists about their cultural competency at the time of the initial intake or consultation is an additional choice. People might question therapists about their strategy to integrating cultural issues into treatment, their knowledge of cultural factors that may influence mental health, and their experience working with clients from a variety of backgrounds. This can assist clients in assessing the cultural competency of their therapist and whether they feel supported and at ease in the therapeutic alliance.

For those in need of mental health services, community organizations, internet forums, and support groups tailored to a particular culture can be excellent sources of information and assistance in addition to individual therapy. These services can help people feel connected, understood, and supported as they walk their healing journey by providing culturally appropriate programming, peer support, and education about mental health concerns within certain groups.

Finding services and therapists who are culturally competent necessitates proactive community lobbying, study, and teamwork. People might obtain the efficient and encouraging mental health treatment they require to recover and flourish by looking for therapists who appreciate and comprehend their cultural backgrounds and identities.

Chapter Seven

REBUILDING SELF-ESTEEM AND SELF-WORTH

This is a critical turning point in the healing process from narcissistic abuse; it's a chapter devoted to taking back control of one's own life and establishing boundaries. This chapter primarily explores the complex process of regaining one's feeling of autonomy and value, which are essential first stages in the healing and reconstruction of one's sense of agency following trauma.

Boundaries are constantly being crossed and one's sense of self and autonomy are being attacked relentlessly are characteristics of narcissistic abuse. Victims frequently become entangled in a web of pressure, manipulation, and gaslighting in which the abuser routinely disregards their needs and boundaries. Regaining one's own power thus turns into a defiant act and a statement of one's value in the face of difficulty.

Setting limits is a key component of self-care and self-preservation, and it is the central idea of this chapter. Setting boundaries entails stating one's wants and preferences, defining clearly defined boundaries for acceptable and undesirable behavior, and safeguarding oneself from additional injury. Setting boundaries can feel like a radical act of self-love for victims of narcissistic abuse, a way to recover agency and autonomy in a society that has routinely disempowered them.

Setting limits is not without its difficulties, though. As they deal with ingrained patterns of people-pleasing and self-sacrifice, victims may struggle with feelings of guilt, humiliation, and self-doubt. They can worry about offending family members or loved ones by voicing their demands and boundaries, or they might fear reprisals or repercussions from the abuser. Setting boundaries is a crucial part of self-care and self-preservation, and survivors who face these obstacles must learn to be resilient and self-compassionate.

Regaining control over one's ideas, feelings, and behaviors is another aspect of regaining personal power. It's possible that victims of narcissistic abuse were socialized to put the abuser's wants and demands ahead of their own, which robbed them of their identity and autonomy. Regaining personal authority entails accepting that one is not accountable for the ideas, feelings, or deeds of others and standing up for one's right to make decisions that are consistent with one's values and objectives.

This chapter also looks at how self-compassion plays a part in regaining personal power and setting boundaries. Self-compassion entails being compassionate, understanding, and accepting of oneself, especially while facing challenges or self-doubt. Survivors need to have the ability to question their own negative beliefs and replace them with narratives that are more affirming and compassionate, acknowledging their intrinsic value and dignity as human beings.

Chapter Eight

HEALING INTERPERSONAL RELATIONSHIPS

This is a critical turning point in the healing process from narcissistic abuse; it's a chapter devoted to taking back control of one's own life and establishing boundaries. This chapter primarily explores the complex process of regaining one's feeling of autonomy and value, which are essential first stages in the healing and reconstruction of one's sense of agency following trauma.

Boundaries are constantly being crossed and one's sense of self and autonomy are being attacked relentlessly are characteristics of narcissistic abuse. Victims frequently become entangled in a web of pressure, manipulation, and gaslighting in which the abuser routinely disregards their needs and boundaries. Regaining one's own power thus turns into a defiant act and a statement of one's value in the face of difficulty.

Setting limits is a key component of self-care and self-preservation, and it is the central idea of this chapter. Setting boundaries entails stating one's wants and preferences, defining clearly defined boundaries for acceptable and undesirable behavior, and safeguarding oneself from additional injury. Setting boundaries can feel like a radical act of self-love for victims of narcissistic abuse, a way to recover agency and autonomy in a society that has routinely disempowered them.

Setting limits is not without its difficulties, though. As they deal with ingrained patterns of people-pleasing and self-sacrifice, victims may struggle with feelings of guilt, humiliation, and self-doubt. They can worry about offending family members or loved ones by voicing their demands and boundaries, or they might fear reprisals or repercussions from the abuser. Setting boundaries is a crucial part of self-care and self-preservation, and survivors who face these obstacles must learn to be resilient and self-compassionate.

Regaining control over one's ideas, feelings, and behaviors is another aspect of regaining personal power. It's possible that victims of narcissistic abuse were socialized to put the abuser's wants and demands ahead of their own, which robbed them of their identity and autonomy. Regaining personal authority entails accepting that one is not accountable for the ideas, feelings, or deeds of others and standing up for one's right to make decisions that are consistent with one's values and objectives.

This chapter also looks at how self-compassion plays a part in regaining personal power and setting boundaries. Self-compassion entails being compassionate, understanding, and accepting of oneself, especially while facing challenges or self-doubt. Survivors need to have the ability to question their own negative beliefs and replace them with narratives that are more affirming and compassionate, acknowledging their intrinsic value and dignity as human beings.

Chapter Nine

EMPOWERING BLACK SURVIVORS

This is a critical turning point in the healing process from narcissistic abuse; it's a chapter devoted to taking back control of one's own life and establishing boundaries. This chapter primarily explores the complex process of regaining one's feeling of autonomy and value, which are essential first stages in the healing and reconstruction of one's sense of agency following trauma.

Boundaries are constantly being crossed and one's sense of self and autonomy are being attacked relentlessly are characteristics of narcissistic abuse. Victims frequently become entangled in a web of pressure, manipulation, and gaslighting in which the abuser routinely disregards their needs and boundaries. Regaining one's own power thus turns into a defiant act and a statement of one's value in the face of difficulty.

Setting limits is a key component of self-care and self-preservation, and it is the central idea of this chapter. Setting boundaries entails stating one's wants and preferences, defining clearly defined boundaries for acceptable and undesirable behavior, and safeguarding oneself from additional injury. Setting boundaries can feel like a radical act of self-love for victims of narcissistic abuse, a way to recover agency and autonomy in a society that has routinely disempowered them.

Setting limits is not without its difficulties, though. As they deal with ingrained patterns of people-pleasing and self-sacrifice, victims may struggle with feelings of guilt, humiliation, and self-doubt. They can worry about offending family members or loved ones by voicing their demands and boundaries, or they might fear reprisals or repercussions from the abuser. Setting boundaries is a crucial part of self-care and self-preservation, and survivors who face these obstacles must learn to be resilient and self-compassionate.

Regaining control over one's ideas, feelings, and behaviors is another aspect of regaining personal power. It's possible that victims of narcissistic abuse were socialized to put the abuser's wants and demands ahead of their own, which robbed them of their identity and autonomy. Regaining personal authority entails accepting that one is not accountable for the ideas, feelings, or deeds of others and standing up for one's right to make decisions that are consistent with one's values and objectives.

This chapter also looks at how self-compassion plays a part in regaining personal power and setting boundaries. Self-compassion entails being compassionate, understanding, and accepting of oneself, especially while facing challenges or self-doubt. Survivors need to have the ability to question their own negative beliefs and replace them with narratives that are more affirming and compassionate, acknowledging their intrinsic value and dignity as human beings.

Chapter Ten

CULTIVATING RESILENCE AND STRENGTH

Black survivors of abuse provide compelling accounts that underscore the fortitude, bravery, and perseverance of individuals who have surmounted hardships and reclaimed their agency. These narratives provide inspiration, validation, and empowerment to individuals who may be confronting comparable obstacles in their personal journeys, serving as a guiding light.

Individuals' ingenuity and resilience in the midst of adversity constitute one of the most extraordinary facets of narratives of triumph and resilience from African American survivors. In the midst of insurmountable obstacles and traumatic experiences, survivors demonstrate a determination not to be defined by their past. Rather, they forge a path towards healing and empowerment by tapping into their inner strength and resilience. Their narratives exemplify the capacity of the human spirit to persevere, adjust, and develop amidst adversity.

Furthermore, narratives of fortitude and success underscore the significance of solidarity and support within the African American community. Numerous survivors attribute their resilience in the face of adversity to the encouragement and support of friends, family, and members of the community who stood by them during their most trying times. These narratives highlight the efficacy of communal support in furnishing survivors with affirmation, compassion, and useful connections throughout their process of recovery.

Moreover, narratives that highlight the fortitude, diversity, and resistance of Black survivors in the midst of systemic injustice and discrimination dispel unfounded preconceived notions and detrimental stereotypes concerning Black communities and individuals. These narratives challenge the prevailing views of victimization and pathology by affirming the humanity, agency, and dignity of African American people who have triumphed over challenges and reclaimed their agency.

In addition, the triumphs and tenacity of African American survivors serve as an impassioned plea for greater social justice and systemic transformation. Through the act of recounting their personal experiences and advocating for changes in policy, survivors effectively magnify their influence, heighten consciousness regarding the widespread occurrence of abuse within the African American community, and enforce responsibility on those responsible as well as the establishments that sustain such damage. These narratives motivate and foster solidarity and collective action, propelling endeavors to establish a more just and nurturing setting that facilitates the recovery and flourishing of survivors.

In summary, the testimonies of African American survivors of abuse serve as compelling illustrations of the fortitude, bravery, and perseverance of people who have conquered hardship and reclaimed their agency. These narratives stimulate endeavors towards social justice and systemic change, challenge detrimental preconceptions and misconceptions, and inspire optimism, validation, and empowerment. Through the act of recounting their personal experiences and advocating for reform, survivors forge a future in which abuse is deemed intolerable, and every individual is embraced and believed in as they navigate the path to recovery and empowerment.

Cultivating a mind-set of resilience in the face of adversity

Developing a mindset characterized by resilience when confronted with adversity is a profoundly empowering endeavor that enables one to effectively navigate obstacles, setbacks, and traumatic experiences with fortitude, fortitude, and persistence. Resilience is a learned and strengthened capacity that can be cultivated and reinforced through deliberate effort, introspection, and adopting a growth-oriented mindset.

A critical element in fostering resilience is the cultivation of a growth mindset, which entails perceiving obstacles and setbacks as chances for personal development and learning, rather than as reflections of inherent capabilities or value. People who possess a growth mindset exhibit inquisitiveness, adaptability, and a positive outlook when confronted with challenges; they perceive setbacks as transitory barriers that can be surmounted through diligence, perseverance, and fortitude. By transforming adversity into a learning and development opportunity, people can cultivate increased resilience and adaptability when confronted with obstacles.

Furthermore, the development of emotional intelligence and self-awareness is integral to the cultivation of resilience, as it enables people to identify and control their emotions when confronted with adversity and duress. Through the adoption of mindfulness practices, such as journaling, meditation, and deep breathing, people have the ability to foster an enhanced awareness of themselves and their presence. This heightened awareness empowers them to confront obstacles with composure, courage, and lucidity. Developing healthy coping mechanisms, such as engaging in physical activity, pursuing creative endeavors, or immersing oneself in natural environments, can further assist people in regulating stress and fostering fortitude when confronted with challenges.

In addition, the cultivation of social connections and supportive relationships is critical in the development of resilience. Individuals who possess robust social support networks exhibit enhanced capacity to manage stress and adversity due to the availability of emotional solace, practical aid, and validation from their social circle, according to research. Through the establishment of substantial connections with loved ones, acquaintances, and members of the community who provide encouragement, solidarity, and empathy, individuals can strengthen their resilience during periods of adversity.

Additionally, in the face of adversity, fostering a sense of purpose, meaning, and optimism is an integral part of developing resilience. Those who possess a distinct sense of purpose and significance in life exhibit greater fortitude and resolve when confronted with obstacles and setbacks. Through the process of identifying their values, passions, and objectives, people have the ability to develop a sense of purpose that serves to motivate and sustain them in the midst of challenges.

In summary, fostering a mindset characterized by resilience when confronted with hardship is a profoundly empowering endeavor that enables people to confront obstacles, setbacks, and traumatic experiences with fortitude, fortitude, and persistence. Individuals can cultivate the resilience necessary to flourish despite challenges by adopting a growth mindset, enhancing their self-awareness and emotional intelligence, being a part of supportive social circles, and developing a sense of purpose and meaning. By engaging in deliberate effort and introspection, people have the ability to develop a mindset characterized by resilience, which enables them to surmount barriers, welcome difficulties, and lead a life filled with bravery, fortitude, and perseverance.

Turning pain into purpose
A transformative process, transforming suffering into purpose entails discovering purpose, development, and self-empowerment throughout

the road to recovery from adversity and trauma. It involves converting the anguish and distress caused by previous encounters into a wellspring of fortitude, perseverance, and intention that drives individual development and constructive transformation.

A critical element in the process of transforming suffering into meaning is reorienting one's outlook on hardship and trauma. Individuals have the capacity to transform their perception of trauma from a mere source of anguish and suffering to a chance for personal development, education, and growth. By adopting an attitude of resilience and empowerment, individuals can reframe their experiences, thereby imbuing their recovery journey with significance and intention. This entails acknowledging that their hardships have contributed to their development as more resilient, enlightened, and empathetic beings.

Furthermore, the process of transforming suffering into meaning requires recognizing and utilizing the potential of narratives and advocacy to effect constructive transformations within oneself and others. By recounting their personal experiences of recuperation and fortitude, people have the ability to motivate and enable others who may be confronted with comparable obstacles. By engaging in advocacy, individuals have the capacity to increase consciousness regarding the widespread occurrence of trauma and abuse, contest societal stigmatization and fallacies, and promote systemic transformation and social equity. Through utilizing their suffering as a stimulus for constructive progress, people have the ability to establish a lasting heritage of fortitude, self-empowerment, and optimism that transcends their personal process of recuperation.

In addition, transforming suffering into motivation necessitates discovering methods to direct one's emotions and experiences towards constructive manifestation and significant behavior. By engaging in community service, writing, art, or activism, individuals can discover healing and self-expression avenues that enable them to reclaim their agency and voice when confronted with adversity. Through the deliberate redirection of their suffering, people have the ability to foster a sense of agency, purpose, and significance in their existence, thereby establishing a trajectory towards recovery and metamorphosis.

In spite of the difficulties and obstacles of the past, fostering an attitude of gratitude and appreciation for the present moment is another component of transforming suffering into purpose. Even when confronted with adversity, individuals can develop resilience, faith, and optimism by concentrating on the positive aspects of life. By adopting the practices of mindfulness and gratitude, people can discover happiness, satisfaction, and meaning in the mundane occurrences of daily existence, acknowledging that even the most dire circumstances harbor opportunities to discover beauty and illumination.

Finding meaning, development, and empowerment along the path to recovery from adversity and trauma constitutes, in summary, the process of transforming suffering into purpose. Through adopting a reframed viewpoint, embracing advocacy and narrative, channeling emotions into creative expression and action, and developing mindfulness and gratitude, people have the ability to transform their suffering into a wellspring of fortitude, perseverance, and direction that drives positive transformation and personal development. By engaging in purposeful practice and introspection, individuals have the ability to imbue their recovery journey with significance and direction, thereby establishing a lasting heritage of fortitude, empowerment, and optimism that motivates and enables others.

About the Author

Gbogo .S. Adegboye is a multifaceted professional, serving as a manager, business economist, entrepreneur, and motivational speaker across Africa. Adegboye boasts bachelor's degrees from Yale University, IPMA, and Adonai University, along with a Master of Business Administration (MBA) from Salfold University, Manchester. While born in South Africa, he currently resides in Nigeria, actively engaging as a motivational speaker in various institutions, industries, and seminars, particularly catering to young and aspiring managers throughout the African continent.

Acknowledgment

In the outset, I would like to express my sincere appreciation to my family, friends, well-wishers, and an innumerable number of individuals whose names I am unable to mention for their consistent support in various capacities, without which the successful completion of this medical manuscript would have been unattainable. Furthermore, I extend my gratitude to God for the guidance that has been a constant source of assistance and sustenance throughout the process.

THANKS FOR READING

www.ingramcontent.com/pod-product-compliance
Lightning Source LLC
Chambersburg PA
CBHW051231120626
46547CB00013B/1599